DO IT YOURSELF

Recycling

Reducing Waste

Buffy Silverman

Heinemann Library
Chicago, Illinois

Customer Service 888-454-2279
Visit our website at www.heinemannraintree.com

Designed by Richard Parker and Tinstar Design Ltd, www.tinstar.co.uk
Printed and bound in China by Leo Paper Group

12 11 10 09
10 9 8 7 6 5 4 3 2

Library of Congress Cataloging-in-Publication Data
Silverman, Buffy.
Recycling : reducing waste / Buffy Silverman.
p. cm. -- (Do it yourself)
Includes bibliographical references and index.
ISBN 978-1-4329-1090-7 (hc) -- ISBN 978-1-4329-1106-5 (pb) 1. Refuse and refuse disposal--Juvenile
literature. 2. Recycling (Waste, etc.)--Juvenile literature. I. Title.
TD792.S56 2008
363.72'82--dc22

2008008452

Acknowledgments
The publishers would like to thank the following for permission to reproduce photographs: ©Alamy
pp. 5 (Design Pics Inc.), 15 (Eurostyle Graphics), 38 (Dominic Burke), 41 (Jim West); ©Corbis pp. 13,
14 (Beateworks/Dana Hoff), 17 (Jose Fuste Raga), 30 (Richard T. Nowitz), 31 (Matt Rainey), 33 (Brand
X/Alison Miksch), 34 (zefa/Hans Neleman); ©DK Images (Andy Crawford) p. 39; ©Getty Images pp. 4
(Stone +), 7 (Taxi), 21 (First Light/Benjamin Rondel); ©Pearson Education Ltd (Tudor Photography)
p. 35; ©Photolibrary pp. 9 (Index Stock Imagery), 16 (Australian Only), 20 (Ypps Ypps), 23 (Flirt
Collection), 37 (It Stock RM); ©Punchstock (Masterfile/Radius Images) p. 43; ©Rex Features (Philippe
Hays) p. 8; ©Science Photo Library pp. 6 (Simon Fraser/Northumbrian Environmental Management
Ltd), 19 (Adam Hart-Davis), 27 (James King-Holmes), 29 (Hank Morgan).

Cover photograph of a stack of newspapers reproduced with permission of ©Corbis (moodboard).

The publishers would like to thank Nick Lapthorn for his help in the preparation of this book.

Every effort has been made to contact copyright holders of any material reproduced in this book.
Any omissions will be rectified in subsequent printings if notice is given to the publishers.

Contents

Any words appearing in the text in bold, **like this**, are explained in the glossary.

Where Does Your Trash Go?

You have just returned from the store, where you have bought a brand new game. You take it out of the plastic bag and toss the bag on the floor. Grabbing some scissors, you cut open a hard plastic case. Inside, you find a layer of cardboard surrounding the game. Finally, you pull it out and are ready to play.

But you are told to clean up the mess before you play your game. You grab the plastic bag, the hard plastic shell, and the cardboard. Should you run to the trash can and throw them away? Or can you find something better to do with your trash?

Stop and think

Before you throw something away, stop to think about what happens to trash. There are many things you can do to **reduce** your waste. When you make the choice to reuse and recycle materials, you help reduce waste.

What can you do with the packaging that comes wrapped around toys?

Taking care of trash

You take the bag and put it with others in a closet. The next time you go to the store, you can bring the bag and **reuse** it. You do not have any use for the cardboard or the plastic, so you put them in your family's recycling bins.

Now you can enjoy your game. It took you an extra minute to clean up. But you don't mind. You have made a choice to reuse and **recycle** your trash. Because of your choice, there will be less garbage heading to a **landfill**.

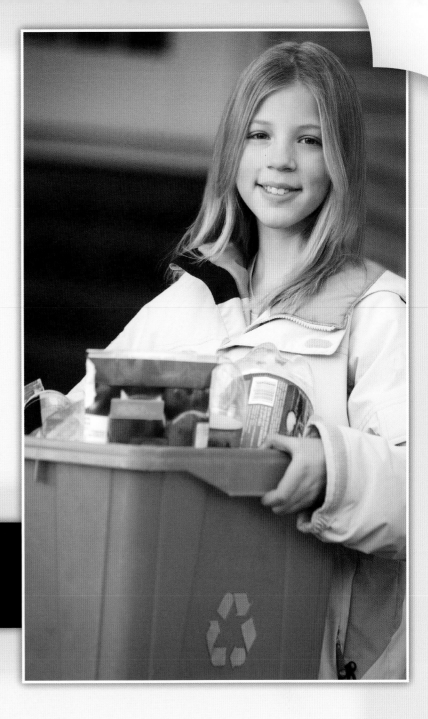

When you recycle packaging, you make less trash.

Making choices

Every day we are faced with choices about how to treat our trash. It is easy to dump what we do not want in the trash and never think about it again. But our trash does not disappear. Mounds and mounds of trash get carted away to landfills. When a landfill is filled with garbage, a new one must be dug. The waste in landfills stays buried for hundreds of years.

Garbage, garbage, and more garbage

People throw things away every day, including newspapers, packages, boxes, and bottles. Small things, such as leftover food, pile up in our trash. Big appliances such as old stoves and refrigerators get thrown out, too.

The trash we dump is called **solid waste**. In the United States, each person throws out an average of 4.5 pounds (2 kilograms) of solid waste per day. That piles up to more than 1,600 pounds (725 kg) of waste per person in a year. In the United Kingdom, people throw out about 1,100 pounds (500 kg) of trash each year. In Beijing, China, the average amount of solid waste per person is about 800 pounds (365 kg) each year.

What happens to solid waste? In the United States, about 66 percent of waste ends up at a landfill. The rest is recycled, made into **compost**, or burned.

Garbage is buried at a landfill.

What is a landfill?

A landfill is a place for disposing waste. A landfill could be a hole in the ground that is dug out, left from a mine or quarry, or a canyon. A landfill could also be a mound where waste is piled above ground. Landfills are usually located near a road and away from homes.

Landfills are built to keep solid waste in place. A **liner** is put underneath the landfill, so waste does not leak out. The liner is made of clay or plastic. It protects the soil and water near a landfill.

Bulldozers compact trash before it is covered with soil.

A landfill is divided into sections. Only a few sections are filled at a time. Garbage trucks at a landfill are checked to make sure they only dump what is allowed in the landfill. A truck is weighed and the garbage company pays for the weight of the load it dumps.

Bulldozers **compact** the trash at the landfill. At the end of each day, the bulldozers cover the garbage on top with soil so it has less exposure to wind and rain. As trash slowly breaks down, gas forms inside the landfill. Pipes allow the gas to escape.

Not in my backyard

What happens to garbage that is dumped in landfills? It sits and sits and sits! Landfills are tightly sealed, so little oxygen and water get in. **Bacteria** and other **organisms** that break things down are called **decomposers**. Most decomposers cannot live in a landfill because they need oxygen and water to survive.

Bulldozers are compacting trash at this landfill.

Track your trash

Where does your community take its trash? Call your city hall or town office and ask about your local landfill. How far away is the landfill? How large is it? Is trash carried by truck, railroad, or barges (a type of boat)?

Long-lasting trash

No one knows for sure how long it takes for garbage to break down in a landfill, but it is a long time. Scientists at the University of Arizona dug up trash from a landfill to see if it had broken down. Newspapers take only about a month to decompose in soil. But in the landfill, they found 30-year-old newspapers that they could still read. The scientists dug up grass clippings, a T-bone steak, and hot dogs that looked the same as when they were thrown out. Paper took up more space in the landfill than anything else. If all the newspapers had been recycled, the landfill would not have filled up as quickly.

As people dump more and more garbage, landfills become full. Many cities face the problem of what to do with their trash. No one wants a new landfill in his or her neighborhood. They think a landfill will bring rats and other pests. They do not want noise and dust from garbage trucks rumbling past. They worry about bad smells and **polluted** water from a landfill.

Garbage trucks travel a long way to take trash to landfills.

When landfills fill up, trash must be transported farther away. Cities spend more money and use more fuel to get rid of their waste.

Steps to follow

Will it rot?

For this activity you will need:

* Four flowerpots of the same size
* Garden soil
* Masking tape
* A pencil
* Newspaper
* A plastic bag
* Foam peanuts or other type of foam
* Vegetable scraps or leaves

1 Using masking tape, label each flowerpot as follows: Paper, Plastic, Foam, Vegetables.

2 Fill the four flowerpots one-third full with soil. Use soil from a garden if possible. The flowerpots will represent landfills.

3 Find a small amount (about the size that can fit in the palm of your hand) of each of these kinds of trash: newspaper; plastic bag; foam (for example, packaging peanuts); and vegetable scraps or leaves.

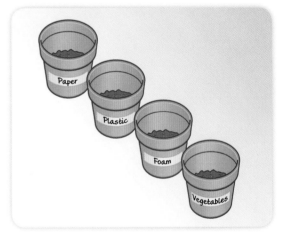

4 Cut or tear each trash sample into small pieces.

5 Scatter the trash over the soil. Put paper in the pot that is labeled Paper; plastic in the pot labeled Plastic; foam in the pot labeled Foam; and vegetable scraps in the pot labeled Vegetables.

6 Cover each pot with soil until it is almost full.

7 Water the soil until it is moist.

8 Place each pot on a shelf in a dark place (for example, a closet.)

9 Once a week, add water to each pot so it is moist.

10 After four weeks, take a look inside your landfills. Spread out four sections of newspaper. Dump out the contents of each pot on a section of paper. Compare what happened to each kind of trash. How do they look different? Which have started to turn to soil? Wash your hands when you are finished.

Take a closer look

Were there fewer paper and vegetable scraps in your pots? Paper and vegetables are **biodegradable**. The decomposers living in soil can break them down in a short time. Plastic is not biodegradable. It takes hundreds of years to break down.

When garbage rots, it becomes part of the soil. The scraps that you buried will break down faster in your pots than at a landfill, though. Inside your pots, decomposers have plenty of air and water. They decompose the paper and vegetables that you buried and turn them into soil.

Talking Trash

What's in your trash?

For this activity you will need:

* Your household trash
* Rubber gloves
* Newspaper
* Trash bags
* A scale
* A calculator
* A notebook and pencil

1 Tell your family you plan to keep track of the trash for two days. Begin by emptying the trash and asking that no one empty it again for the next two days.

2 Collect all the trash that your family makes for the next two days. Do not collect yard waste, construction waste, or any chemical waste.

3 Ask a parent where you can sort your trash and spread out plenty of newspapers. Wearing rubber gloves, sort the trash into these categories; glass, paper, food waste, plastic, cardboard, metal, and miscellaneous (anything that cannot be classified in the above groups).

4 Label individual bags for each category. Use a sealable bag for food waste.

5 Weigh the amount of waste in each bag. Record what you find in a notebook.

6 Add the total weight of the garbage that your household produced. Divide by two to calculate the average waste per day.

7 Multiply your average daily waste by seven. The result will give you an idea of the amount of waste your household produces in one week.

8 Multiple your average weekly waste by 52. The result will give you an idea of the amount of waste your household produces in one year.

What next?

Share the results of your survey with the rest of your household. Did you find items in the trash that you could **recycle**? The people in your household could also **compost** food waste. Were there items in your trash that could be **reused**? Discuss how you can **reduce** waste with other members of your household.

In most communities, glass, paper, plastic, cardboard, and metal can be recycled.

Recycling—a way to reduce your trash

Would you throw money in the trash? When people throw out paper and glass, that is basically what they are doing. It costs money for the materials and **energy** used to make paper and glass. By recycling, you save energy, materials, and money.

Recycling tip

When buying new things, check to see if they are made of recycled materials. If you have a choice, always buy recycled products.

A truck picks up materials for recycling from curbside bins.

What is recycling?

When things are recycled, they are reused to make new products. Old paper is used to make new paper. Glass is melted down and made into new bottles and jars. Aluminum, iron, plastics, batteries, and other materials are also recycled. Food waste and yard waste is recycled by composting.

Recycling helps the **environment**. Through recycling, people reduce the amount of energy and **resources** used to make things. By using less energy, less air and water pollution is created. We send less trash to the **landfill**. About 75 percent of what we throw away could be recycled. Today, only 25 percent of those materials are actually recycled.

What would happen if four families in your neighborhood recycled all the paper they used for one year? That would save 20 trees that otherwise would be cut to make paper. Enough energy would be saved to power your home for six months!

You can recycle

Save what you can for recycling. Paper, glass, plastic and other materials are separated. Then they are brought to a recycling station. The old materials are sold to factories that make new materials.

Some communities have curbside recycling, with trucks that pick up recycled materials at your home. Other communities have recycling stations where you can bring materials for recycling.

Recycling where you live

What can you recycle? Call your town, city, or county offices and find out what material can be recycled in your community. Is recycling picked up at your home? Is there a recycling station nearby?

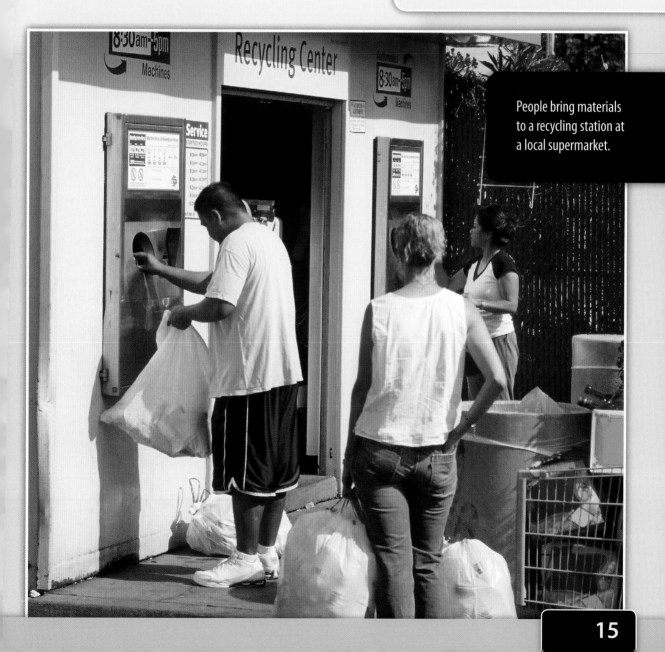

People bring materials to a recycling station at a local supermarket.

Recycle It!

How many food and beverage cans are in your kitchen? Altogether, Americans use more than 130 billion metal cans a year. About 80 billion of these cans are made of aluminum. Aluminum is the most abundant metal on Earth. It is part of a **mineral** called **bauxite** that is mined from the earth's crust.

People discovered aluminum in the 1820s. Today, aluminum is used to make cans, buildings, cars, computers, and other things. Aluminum is long lasting and easy to **recycle**. More than two-thirds of the aluminum ever produced is still in use.

Aluminum is made from bauxite, a mineral that is mined from the earth.

Aluminum recycling

More than half of all aluminum cans are recycled, which means they do not go to a **landfill**. Aluminum can be recycled over and over again. The aluminum in a single can may have been used many times before. Many recycled materials must be mixed with new material when products are made. But recycled aluminum does not need to be mixed with new aluminum. New cans can be made completely out of material from old cans. This is called **closed-loop recycling**. In about 60 days, a used aluminum can can be recycled, refilled, and put back on the shelf of a grocery store.

New cans can be made from old ones when they are recycled.

Making a new can from recycled aluminum takes much less **energy** than making a can from bauxite. With the energy needed to make one new can from bauxite, 20 cans can be made from recycled aluminum. Recycling one can saves enough energy to run a television for three hours or to light a bulb for four hours. Every can that is thrown away wastes energy and **pollutes** Earth.

Paying for recycling

Many communities pay for their curbside pick-up programs with money earned from selling aluminum cans.

How is a can recycled?

For this activity you will need:

* Canned foods
* Scrap paper
* A magnet

1 Use a magnet to discover how cans are sorted before they are recycled. Take out a variety of cans from your kitchen.

2 Label three pieces of scrap paper: A, B, C. Put each label on the table.

3 Test each can with a magnet. Does the magnet stick to all parts of the can? If so, put the can by the scrap paper labeled A. Does the magnet stick to the sides, but not the ends of the can? Put it by the label B. Is there no attraction between the magnet and the can? Put it by the label C.

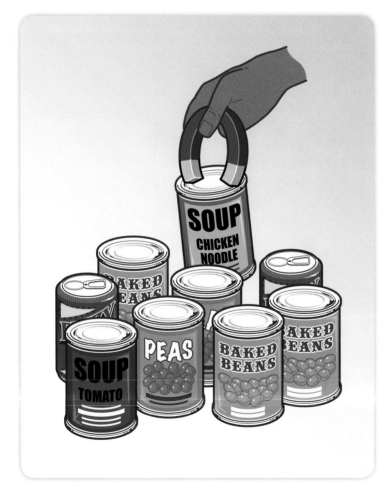

What is in each pile?

The cans by the A label are made of steel. Steel is attracted to a magnet. The bodies of the cans by the B label are made of steel, and the ends are made of aluminum. A magnet does not attract aluminum. Pile C contains cans that are made only of aluminum.

At a recycling plant, cans are sorted in the same way. Huge magnets separate aluminum from steel. Then the aluminum and steel are compressed into bricks. The bricks are sent to separate factories to be recycled and turned into new products.

Aluminum is shredded, crushed, and burned to remove labels and decorations. When the pieces of aluminum are small scraps, they are melted in a furnace. Liquid aluminum is poured into 25-foot- (7.5-meter-) long bars. The thick bars are pressed into thin sheets that can be rolled up into coils. These are shipped to factories that use aluminum.

Steel is recycled in a similar way. The thin layer of tin that coats a steel can is removed and sold to a tin recycler. The steel is then melted in a furnace and rolled and flattened into sheets. Recycled steel is used to make cars, beams for buildings, and new cans.

Recycled aluminum is made into cans, pie pans, siding for houses, small appliances, and lawn furniture.

Recycling Paper

Every day you use paper. You read books printed on paper. At breakfast, you might pour cereal from boxes made of paper. At school you open a notebook and write on paper. On a family trip, you take photographs and print them on paper. You read newspapers and books made of paper.

People throw away a lot of paper. For every 100 pounds (45 kg) of trash thrown away, 35 pounds (15.75 kg) is paper. In a typical **landfill**, newspapers take up 14 percent of the space. Paper packaging uses 15 to 20 percent. The easiest way to save landfill space is by throwing out less paper.

Don't throw out paper! Instead, recycle it. Recycled paper saves trees and energy.

Making paper

Paper is made from the fibers that make plants strong. Most paper is made from trees. Huge forests of spruce, pine, fir, and other trees are grown for making wood **pulp**. Pulp is the fluffy fibers that make up wood. After trees are cut and the bark is removed, wood is crushed and soaked. It is cooked until it looks like a stew. Chemicals are often added to turn the pulp smooth and white. Pulp is shaped on wire **mesh**, so the water drains out. Then it is rolled into paper and dried.

Paper pulp can also be made from **recycled** paper. But today, 90 percent of pulp used for paper comes from trees. If everyone recycled their Sunday newspapers, 500,000 trees could be saved each Sunday.

These bundles of paper are ready for recycling.

Paper cannot be recycled over and over like aluminum. The fibers in pulp get shorter each time they are recycled. Most paper can be recycled four to six times. Usually recycled pulp is mixed with new wood pulp to make paper stronger.

It takes about 40 percent less **energy** to make paper from recycled pulp. Recycled paper uses less water and makes less pollution. When we recycle paper, less waste ends up at landfills.

New paper from old paper

1 Schools and offices use a lot of paper. Brainstorm ways that your class can use less paper. Can you print on both sides of a sheet of paper? Set up a bin for scrap paper that you can **reuse** before it is recycled. How else can you save paper? Challenge your classmates to **reduce** the amount of paper that you use.

2 Find out what kinds of paper you can recycle and where they should be taken. Does the paper need to be sorted by type?

3 Set up and label bins for recycling. If your recycling program requires that paper be sorted, put out different bins for different types of paper: newsprint, paperboard, cardboard, and office paper. Try to keep all paper out of your classroom's trash.

What next?

People have been recycling paper for as long as they have used it. You can recycle paper at home and at school. Encourage your household to use less paper and recycle paper waste.

Recycling paper

At a recycling center, paper is wrapped into **bales.** Then it is sold to a paper mill. There, a conveyer belt moves paper into a pulper. The pulper contains water and chemicals. Old paper is chopped into tiny pieces. Scraps from the mill's papermaking process are also chopped and added to the mix. The wet scraps are heated until they form a mush, also called pulp.

The pulp is forced through screens and then spun through a cylinder. The spinning removes glue, staples, and bits of plastic that might be mixed in. The pulp is washed to remove any ink. Then, it is beaten to make the fibers swell. Chemicals are used to remove dyes from colored papers. The pulp is whitened with bleach.

Finally, the clean pulp is ready to make paper. It can be used alone or blended with new wood fibers. Often recycled pulp is mixed with wood pulp so that the paper will be stronger.

Recycled paper is taken to a paper mill.

Steps to follow

Warning: Ask an adult to help you with this activity.

1 Put on some old clothes. Take two pieces of writing paper from a recycling bin. Remove any plastic, tape, or staples. Tear the paper into small pieces. Soak the pieces in a bowl of hot water for half an hour.

2 Fill a blender half full with warm water. Add a handful of soaked paper. Blend until the paper disappears.

3 Add three or four small pieces of broccoli to the blender. Instead of using wood fibers, you are adding broccoli fibers to strengthen your paper. Blend until the broccoli is mixed in.

4 Put one section of newspaper on the table and place one piece of blotting paper on the newspaper. The mixture should be the consistency of thin oatmeal. Add more water if it is too thick and then mix it by hand.

5 Pour the pulp into the pan. Slide the screen into the pan. As you lift the screen, it should be completely covered with pulp. Spread it evenly with your fingers.

Making paper

For this activity you will need:

* Paper from your recycling bin
* A bowl of hot water
* A blender
* Broccoli
* A piece of window screen about 5 inches (12.5 cm) square
* A pan that is larger than the screen
* Blotting paper
* Newspaper
* A jar or rolling pin

6 Let the water drain through the screen into the pan. Set the screen on the blotting paper and newspaper. Cover the screen with the second piece of blotting paper and the newspaper.

7 Using a jar or rolling pin, press out the excess water. Remove the top piece of newspaper.

8 Flip over the entire stack. Remove the newspaper, blotting paper, and screen that are now on top. You now have only pulp on top of one piece of blotting paper.

9 Let your pulp dry on the remaining piece of blotter for two hours. Gently peel the paper off and let it dry overnight. How will you use your recycled paper?

More Things to Recycle

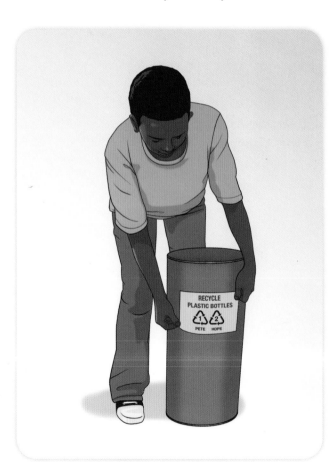

Recycling plastic

For this activity you will need:

* Plastic bottles
* A recycling bin
* A marking pen

1 Call your local recycling agency to find out what types of plastic your community **recycles**.

2 Plastic bottles are labeled with numbers. The numbers refer to the type of plastic.

3 Look at the plastic bottles in your kitchen to find the numbers on them. Which ones can be recycled?

4 Set up a bin for your household's plastic recycling, labeling it with the numbers that can be recycled.

5 Tell members of your household what you have learned about recycling plastic. Show them where to find numbers on plastic bottles and which ones they can recycle.

These plastic pellets have been made from recycled plastic. They can now be used to make new products.

Plastic process

In factories plastics are made from **petroleum** and **natural gas**. Some plastics are thin and flexible. Others are thick and hard. Although it seems like plastics are everywhere, you will find less plastic in a **landfill** than paper. About 11 percent of waste taken to a landfill is plastic, compared to 35 percent paper.

Plastic can be recycled. Soft drink bottles and other plastics are melted down to make plastic resin. The resin is made into carpet, stuffing for ski jackets, car parts, lumber, flowerpots, and new soda bottles.

Today, only about 5 percent of all plastics are recycled. In the past, it was often less expensive to make new plastic than to recycle old plastic. Petroleum was inexpensive. Now the cost of petroleum has risen and more companies want to use recycled plastics.

Recycling glass

For this activity you will need:

* Recycling bins
* Used glass bottles and jars

1 Find out how glass is collected for recycling in your community.

2 Remove the lids from used glass bottles and jars.

3 Wash out the bottles and jars.

4 Place them in a recycling bin, sorting by color if necessary.

5 Recycle only bottles and jars. Do not put lightbulbs, dishes, windowpanes, or broken glass in your glass-recycling bin.

Solid color

Often glass must be sorted by color—clear, green, and brown. The color in bottles cannot be removed when it is recycled, so colored glass cannot be made into clear glass.

What is glass?

People have been making glass for more than 4,500 years. Glass is made from sand, limestone, and **soda ash**. These materials are melted together so they flow like a liquid. Hot liquid glass can be blown to shape it or poured into molds. Glass hardens when it cools.

New glass can also be made from recycled glass. Instead of melting sand, limestone, and soda ash, crushed glass is melted. The crushed glass, called cullet, melts at a lower temperature than raw materials. Because of this, it takes 40 percent less **energy** to make glass from recycled glass than to make new glass.

Recycled glass is made into new jars and bottles. It is also used to make insulation for buildings. Glass can be recycled over and over again.

Recycled glass is crushed before it is melted and made into new bottles.

Reuse it!

Before glass is recycled, you or someone you know could **reuse** it. You can reuse jars for a number of purposes, such as storing leftover food. In some places, if you buy a bottle, you pay a **deposit** on the bottle. To get your money back, you return the bottle to the store. The bottle is then cleaned and refilled. It takes less energy to wash and refill a bottle than to make a new bottle with recycled glass. Eleven states in the United States, many Canadian provinces, and some countries in Europe have deposit laws.

Batteries, cell phones, and computers

Before you buy something new, consider how long you will use it. Will you still want to play the latest electronic game next year? Or will it become one more piece of waste buried in a landfill? If we **reduce** what we buy, we make less waste.

How many games and toys do you have that use batteries? Americans buy nearly three billion batteries a year.

Recycle cell phones

There are many places to recycle cell phones. Stores that sell cell phones collect them for recycling. Cities and towns have places to recycle dangerous wastes, including cell phones and computers. Some have special days to recycle computers.

By recycling batteries, you can keep dangerous chemicals from polluting water and soil.

Rechargeable batteries

You can reduce the number of batteries you use by buying rechargeable batteries. A rechargeable battery can be plugged into a charger and used over and over again. One rechargeable battery can save buying hundreds of single-use batteries.

Eventually rechargeable batteries wear out. What happens to them? Batteries should be recycled. If a battery contains mercury, cadmium, or lead, it is against the law to throw it in the trash. (Alkaline batteries do not contain these substances.) Harmful metals can leak out of old batteries. When they leak, the metals **pollute** water and soil. They should not be sent to a landfill.

Find out where batteries can be recycled in your community. Label a container for storing old batteries and ask your parents to bring them for recycling.

Reuse it

Instead of being recycled, some computers are donated to schools and other groups that need them. First, the computer is checked to make sure it works well. Parts are repaired or replaced. When a school receives a donated computer, it is ready to run.

This computer recycling center dismantles old computers and recycles the parts.

Recycling food and yard waste

For this activity you will need:

* Wire screen
* Yard waste
* Kitchen waste
* A shovel
* Gardening gloves

1 Ask an adult if there is a place where you can make a **compost** pile to recycle food scraps and yard waste. Choose a corner that is out of view from your home or away from your school.

2 Put your gardening gloves on. Ask an adult to help you make a simple frame for your compost pile using the wire screen. It can be square shaped or circular. The frame should be about 3 feet (1 meter) square.

3 **Bacteria** and other **decomposers** will turn your waste into compost. Decomposers need food, water, and air to thrive. In the frame, place a 6-inch (15-cm) layer of brown plant material, such as dead leaves or pine needles. Brown material adds **carbon** to your compost.

4 Sprinkle the brown layer with water.

5 Next, add a 3-inch (7.5-cm) layer of green material. Weeds and grass clippings are good green plant material. Green plant material adds **nitrogen**.

6 Kitchen waste is also good green material, including scraps of fruits, vegetables, coffee grounds, and tea bags. Do not save any meat or dairy products. They will attract pests to your pile. Sprinkle the green layer with water.

7 Add a shovel full of soil to your pile. The soil contains **organisms** that break down dead plants.

8 With your shovel, mix the layers together.

9 As you collect more waste, continue adding layers of brown and green waste to your pile and watering it. Add twice as much brown waste as green waste. Every two weeks, mix your pile with a shovel. Mixing the pile adds air to the lower layers and will speed up the time it takes to compost your waste. If you do not mix your pile, you will still get compost, but it will take six months or more.

10 When your frame is full, start a new compost pile.

11 Add compost to soil whenever you plant anything. Through composting, you save landfill space and help plants grow!

Food scraps and yard waste can be recycled in a compost pile.

Recycling for tomorrow

Every day we throw out a lot of garbage. Some of the materials that we throw out can be reused. Others can be recycled into new products. When we look closely at what we throw out, we can discover new uses for our trash.

That is just what 14-year-old Michael Montelongo did. Michael lived near a factory that processed 300,000 pairs of jeans a week. The factory was left with several million tons of lint. Throwing away the lint cost the company a lot of money. The lint also took up a lot of landfill space.

Michael Montelongo discovered that lint from a jean factory made plants grow better.

A recycling experiment

Michael heard about the huge piles of lint. He wondered if there was some way to recycle it. He decided to experiment with using it as a fertilizer.

Michael planted several kinds of plant. He planted some with just soil and some with lint and soil. He measured how well the plants grew and compared them. He also looked at how the lint decomposed and if it changed the soil after one year.

Michael found that lint helped plants grow. Plants grown in soil mixed with lint were healthier and needed less water than those grown just with soil. Why did the lint help the plants? When Michael looked at the soil after one year, he found that the cotton in the lint had released **minerals** when it decomposed. He also found that the soil mixed with lint had made more air spaces. That meant that the soil held water longer and did not need to be watered as often.

Michael showed that using lint as a fertilizer was a good idea. He also showed how kids can find new ways to recycle.

Think about the waste in your home, school, and community. What can you recycle? Can you find a new use for something people throw out?

You can reuse glass jars by keeping things in them instead of throwing them away.

Making Less Trash

What's in a package?

For this activity you will need:

* Groceries that your household uses

1 Offer to put groceries away after a shopping trip. But first, take a look at the packaging.

6 In the final pile, include nonrecyclable containers and wrappers that will be put in the trash. Styrofoam and some other plastics will be here.

2 Make one pile of groceries that have no packaging. Include fresh fruits and vegetables with no extra bags.

3 Make another pile of bottles that you can return to the store, such as glass or plastic bottles with a **deposit**. When you return them, they will be **reused** or **recycled**. Skip this step if you live where there is no deposit on bottles.

4 Make a third pile that includes food packed in containers that you can clean and reuse at home. Tins and some plastic containers can be reused.

Making less trash

How can you cut down your trash? Look at the items with nonrecyclable containers. Can they be packaged in a way that would **reduce** trash? Can you buy items that need little or no packaging? What items can you buy that have reusable or recyclable packages?

5 In the fourth pile place packages that your community recycles. Include glass and plastic bottles, cardboard boxes, and metal cans.

Using less

Speak with others about ways to use less packaging. Discuss these tips. What other ideas do you have to reduce your trash?

Bring cloth bags with you when you go to the store for packing groceries.

Save any paper or plastic bags that you get at a store. Bring them back for another trip home.

Buy items in bulk. One large carton of juice makes less trash than many small juice boxes.

Reuse containers that you bring home instead of buying plastic bags for trash and storage.

What choices can you make when shopping to reduce the amount of packaging you throw out?

Treasures from trash

Marilyn Brackney was worried about the trash that she saw all around her. She knew that **landfills** were filling up and wanted to encourage people to recycle. So, she created Trashasaurus Rex.

Trashasaurus Rex is a sculpture covered with hundreds of pieces of **solid waste**. When neighbors heard about her project, they brought her old toys, watches, and other items that would have gone to a landfill. Brackney used bottle tops, sunglasses, and fly swatters to decorate the brightly colored dinosaur.

Trashasaurus Rex's feet stand in worn-out old boots. Instead of plates on his back, he wears old, mismatched gloves. A mask with wiggly eyes makes it look like he has eyes on the back of his head.

Trashasaurus Rex traveled to remind people around the country to recycle. Now he lives at the Rocky Mount Children's Museum in North Carolina.

Sculptures made of trash remind people to reuse and recycle.

Wrap it up

You can also use recycled materials to make your own gift bags and wrapping paper. Decorate bags from the grocery store with markers. Cut out colorful pictures from magazines and cover a paper bag with them. Or wrap a gift with newspaper. After you've wrapped up your gift, add a card that you've made from your recycled treasures.

Make it yourself

Make a one-of-a-kind sculpture from recycled materials. Instead of buying paper and other art supplies, use materials that might have been thrown out. Save materials in a box and see what you can create.

Here are some ideas of materials to save:

- Tubes from paper towels, toilet paper, wrapping paper
- Cereal boxes, tissue boxes, etc.
- Egg cartons
- Boxes from appliances
- Old wrapping paper
- Magazines

- Brochures
- Calendars
- Greeting cards
- Newspapers
- Add some scissors and tape, and you can create your own masterpiece!

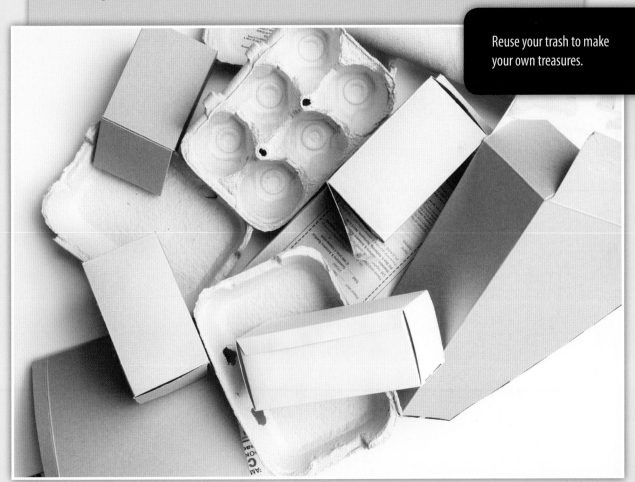

Reuse your trash to make your own treasures.

Landfills for tomorrow

We can reduce the amount of trash that we send to landfills by reusing and recycling. But we still will have some waste, and we will still need a place to store our waste. Some landfills are being redesigned so our garbage takes up less space. They are also being made to produce something useful.

Bioreactor landfills

Most landfills are designed to hold waste in place. In the past, that has meant that there is little air and water in the landfill. The liquid that passes through a landfill, called **leachate**, sits on the **liner** at the bottom until it is removed. Without air and water, most **decomposers** cannot live. Trash breaks down slowly.

New landfills are being designed to encourage decomposition. They are called **bioreactors**. In some, air is pumped into the landfill. The leachate is pumped from the bottom of the landfill into a storage tank. Then it is pumped back into the landfill, passing over the trash many times. With air and liquid pumped in, decomposers break down the trash. As old trash is broken down, there is more space to bury new trash.

Another type of bioreactor landfill works without air. It relies on **bacteria** that do not need air, called **anaerobic bacteria**. Leachate and other liquids pass through the landfill to help decompose wastes, creating more space to bury trash. As the anaerobic bacteria break down waste, they give off **methane** gas. Methane can be used as an **energy** source.

Aerobic Bioreactor

Liquid storage tank

Air blower

■ Air forced into landfill
☐ Leachate removed from the bottom layer of the landfill

In a bioreactor landfill, trash breaks down more quickly.

Landfill gas

In any landfill, methane gas builds up as waste rots. Some landfills burn methane gas to get rid of it. But that **pollutes** the air and impacts the climate. At some landfills, methane gas is collected and sold as fuel. It can also be burned to make steam for heat or electricity. There are more than 400 landfill sites in the United States and Canada that collect and use landfill gas.

Methane gas collected from decaying garbage can be used as fuel to make electricity.

Reduce, Reuse, Recycle

Every day people throw out piles of trash they create at home, work, and school. Groceries, games, clothes, and most goods we buy come wrapped in packaging that fills our garbage cans. When we are done with something, we often throw it in the trash. We lose the materials used to make what we throw away. We lose the **energy** that was needed to make it. Our trash fills huge **landfills** and harms the **environment**.

Reduce

We can all help **reduce** the mountain of trash that we send to landfills. The first step is to think before you buy. Can you use your backpack for another year instead of buying a new one? Can you use one refillable drinking bottle instead of drinking store-bought bottled water? Do you need to own the newest game or music player? Can you share something with a family member or friend instead of buying it for yourself?

Reuse

Instead of throwing out what you no longer need, decide how you can **reuse** it. Would someone you know want a toy that you no longer play with? If you have clothes that are too small, can you give them to someone else to wear? Can you make something new out of the materials in something old? When we reuse things, we make less trash.

Recycle

Many of the things that we throw away can be **recycled**. Huge stacks of newspapers and junk mail fill our landfills. Instead of dumping papers in the trash, recycle them. You can recycle glass, plastic, and aluminum, too. At home and at school, you can encourage others to recycle. As our recycling bins fill, our mountains of trash grow smaller.

All of us must play a part in solving our trash problem. By reducing, reusing, and recycling, we can save energy, make less pollution, and help the Earth.

You can make a difference when you start a recycling program.

Glossary

anaerobic bacteria bacteria that can live without oxygen. Anaerobic bacteria can decompose trash in a landfill.

bacteria tiny one-celled life-form

bale large package of material tied with twine or wire. Newspaper is wrapped in bales and sent to a mill for recycling.

bauxite rock that is mined to make aluminum

biodegradable able to be broken down by living things. Yard waste and vegetable scraps are biodegradable.

bioreactor landfill that is designed so that materials can decompose

carbon chemical element that is in all living things

closed-loop recycling recycling process where new products are made completely from recycled material

compact crush and pack closely together. Bulldozers compact trash at a landfill.

compost mixture of decayed matter that can be used to help plants grow. When you compost food scraps, you recycle them.

decomposer organism that breaks down dead plants or animals. Bacteria, fungi, and worms are decomposers.

deposit sum of money given when bottles are purchased. When you return empty bottles to a store, you receive your deposit back.

energy source of power. Fossil fuel, electricity, and solar power are different kinds of energy.

environment air, water, minerals, plants, and animals that surround a living thing

landfill large, outdoor area used for garbage disposal. The trash that you throw away is taken to a landfill.

leachate liquid that drips through soil or landfills. Leachate has chemicals dissolved in it.

liner clay or plastic material at the bottom of a landfill. A liner keeps materials from leaking out.

mesh interlocking wires with evenly spaced openings. Paper pulp is lifted onto a mesh and the liquid drains out.

methane gas that can be burned and used as a fuel

mineral substance obtained from rocks by mining. Bauxite is a mineral that is mined from the earth.

natural gas fuel that exists as a gas and can be burned for heat, cooking, and to make electricity

nitrogen chemical element that is found in the air, soil, and in plants and animals

organism living thing

petroleum oily liquid that is drilled from the ground and burned as a fuel

pollute make unclean. People worry that landfills create polluted air and water.

pulp soft, moist mass that can be made of paper, wood, or other plant matter. Pulp is made into paper.

recycle take unwanted material and make something useful out of it

reduce use less

resource raw material used to make things

reuse use again. When we reuse materials, we make less waste.

soda ash powdery white chemical used to make glass

solid waste garbage. By recycling, we reduce our solid waste.

Find Out More

Books

Inskipp, Carol. *Reducing and Recycling Waste*. Milwaukee: Gareth Stevens, 2005.

> This book explores more ways to reduce, reuse, and recycle waste.

Martin, Laura C. *Recycled Crafts Box*. North Adams, Mass.: Storey Kids, 2003.

> This books includes 40 earth-friendly projects and activities you can do.

Spilsbury, Louise. *A Sustainable Future*. Chicago: Raintreee, 2006.

> This book discusses how to save and recycle Earth's resources.

Wilcox, Charlotte. *Recycling*. Minneapolis: Lerner, 2007.

> This book describes some interesting ways of turning trash into something useful.

Websites

Recycling IQ Game
www.pacleanways.org/kids
Play a game that tests your knowledge of trash trivia.

Just for Kids
www.depweb.state.pa.us/justforkids
Learn lots of ways to reduce, reuse, and recycle, and play a few games.

Rechargeable Battery Recycling Corporation
www.rbrc.org/call2recycle/dropoff/index.php
Find a place to recycle or safely dispose of your batteries.

Organizations

U.S. Environmental Protection Agency
Ariel Rios Building
1200 Pennsylvania Avenue, N.W.
Washington, DC 20460
(202) 272-0167

www.epa.gov

This organization works for a cleaner, healthier environment through its 10 regional offices and headquarters in Washington, DC.

Kids for a Clean Environment
2804 Foster Avenue
Nashville, TN 37210
(615) 331-7381

www.kidsface.org

Join with other kids to make a difference in your community.

Places to visit

The Rocky Mount Children's Museum and Science Center
270 Gay Street
Rocky Mount, NC 27804
(252) 972-1167

www.rockymountnc.gov/museum

The Rocky Mount Children's Museum and Science Center aims to raise awareness of the connection kids have with the planet. You can see Trashasuarus Rex here.

Index